LOVER, WHERE
ARE YOUR EYES?

LOVER, WHERE ARE YOUR EYES?

ASHA NAZNIN

RECENT
WORK
PRESS

Lover, Where Are Your Eyes?
Recent Work Press
Canberra, Australia

Copyright © Asha Naznin, 2024

ISBN: 9780645973266 (paperback)

Cover design: Recent Work Press
Set by Recent Work Press

recentworkpress.com

SS

For Jacqui Malins

There were days when I was so small and
I didn't have much money, but a true friend

        She, this tall lady, would wait with a drink
        and listen to my poems until after its end

There were days when I wasn't entirely happy
with a piece that I had finished writing

        She, this great lady, would spend her evening
        on me, with her unpaid coaching & editing

Contents

MARILYN MONROE

LOVE & NO SENSE

LOVER

HOME POLITICS

SOLITARY SONG

MARILYN MONROE

Excerpts from Marilyn Monroe's Notebook, 1962

first, the President fell for me, then his brother;
I ended as a body in a bed—classified.

pray no one falls for the things you love:
your land, your lakeshore, ducks whistling for a moment,
your forest, your yellow wattle trees, ancient solace
of red-eyed choughs, angels flocking in black feathers
for a moment, your white home, flying dandelions
smiling in your wind in Spring;
own these delights in your living

with or without your (wo)man.

The Naked Eyes

I wear sunglasses so that I can
look at him straight, and am loud
so he won't notice
the shameless lady
around

But why do you, stupid?

He appeared one afternoon with a pair of naked blue eyes
on Nusa Dua beach in Bali
29 days, 36 minutes and 15 seconds ago!

'Hallelujah!' someone exclaimed into the air—
'Here is the handsome man with those mysterious eyes'
Turning his head slightly back, he smiled at her
as if Marilyn Monroe was dancing,
dancing before her lover: the moment gave birth to
the English idiom 'out of the blue'!

What if I said to him,
your eyes are sweeter than Sumbanese coffee
your eyes are sweeter than Turkish delight
your eyes are sweeter than Indian Golab Jamun

Would you stop for a while and smile back at me?

The next morning,
as if I was a robber,
he began to hide his treasure

Marilyn Monroe, the lady he smiled at, gossiped to everyone:
'His Mama bought him fancy sunglasses to protect him from all those wrinkles
Doesn't he realise Mama's trick? Isn't she keeping girls away
by covering his sweet eyes?'

Why do you hide your sexy eyes inside the hotel, honey?
We don't live in medieval society, do we?

If this were an episode of the Arabian Nights,
I would be after Aladdin's magic ring
to ask the Jinn to fulfil my three wishes:

—Jinni, give the sunglasses back to his Mama
—Jinni, put some clothes on this duplicate Marilyn Monroe
—Jinni, bring the man to me naked!

Well, I mean with naked eyes only
I don't mean anything else;
(it's not necessary to call the police)

Umm, the thing is, before it's too late,
I must see his blue sparkling eyes for one more afternoon,
and many more evenings. In fact, every morning
I must wake up next to those two blue oceans
and sink into their dream until my last breath!

He doesn't know coffee is too bitter nowadays;
Golab Jamuns are rotten,
Turkish delight has lost its flavour.

Only you can bring everything back, darling!

And, let me drink
let me taste
let me smell some sweetness

I bet I will be better than any other Marilyn Monroes
I promise I will never sing to the US President
I guarantee I will never ever take my clothes off
before Donald Trump
on his birthday

I promise this only for you!

LOVE & NO SENSE

A Caged Dentist

It would be unethical
to make any comment
on how sweet you smell
or how mysterious your long hair is;
how dramatic it was
when you moved your hair real estate from your back
to the front of your arm just using your fingers
before lying on the dentist's chair
before me.

I don't dare to comment on how magical it was
as I am a dentist
I can only say to you
'Open your mouth, thank you'
then you did and I saw your pink tongue
and again I cannot comment
as I am your dentist
except to say
'close your mouth, thank you'

But can I say your tonsils were looking nice?
Making comment even on your lips, sorry, I mean mouth,
would be unethical
let alone legs, hips, or knees—
that's what they say,
but what if I say you are the only woman whose tonsils
are enough,
more than enough
to fall in love with?

May I, at least, thank you for letting me see your tonsils?

Since you left my clinic, I have been wondering
who is the lucky ENT specialist who gets to see your tonsils?
If that guy praises your teeth,
don't believe a single word
You've got terrible teeth. Let me fix that right away!
Some might say dentists are robbers—they make you bankrupt
I will bankrupt myself
in making sure you get life-long treatment!

Come and see me every week.
even better, every day!

I repeat, your tonsils are magical, big, pink,
enough, more than enough

to fall in love with,
do you get me?

NB: before I finish my prescription,
I have a little advice about your tongue
Next time you visit me, please don't move
your tongue so much—it distracts me,
as it would almost all single dentists.
Please don't take me to court
claiming that I have no moral values
I do, I do!
Things I've never felt before
with any patient; things started to fall apart
even before I looked at your teeth

It's entirely the fault of God

who made you as magical as a unicorn
who made you walk to me
Next time, no smile please,
with those terrible teeth, I mean

Keep your mouth closed, thank you!

The Mantra Behind My Grade

I did not pass the exam. It's not that I did not study—
it's because he sat before me
in the exam hall.

But there was no news alert on the TV or local radio
The Australian Bureau of Meteorology often doesn't warn the public
with safety messages such as 'Do not sit next to your crush'
As such, in the exam hall, an earthquake was felt,
magnitude 7.5
I could not write a single word
I fainted.

The next semester, I got a high distinction
It's not because the bloody lecturer was damn good
It's not because Floriade was going on in the city
It's because on the morning of the exam,
my crush, who had already graduated, got me a coffee
and walked me to the exam hall
and he said 'You look beautiful.'

Love in the Time of Coronavirus

Tom Cruise
takes his seat
before me
I can't take my eyes off him
what a stunner
I feel like taking
all of my clothes
off entirely

hailstorm
in my head
acting cool
staying calm
along with
my fixed grin
to him

while having our
lime and salt dressed margaritas
on a first date!
how can a single woman
resist spending the night
with such a fit man?
oh my Tom Cruise!
every single day I act
like a feminist—who cares
if tonight I turn out
to be an opportunist!
The Queen of Love

has just been reborn
inside me; like a long-lost rose
just started blooming!

he stares, 'it's so nice
of you
to give me some
of your time'

Jesus! Moses! Muhammad! Buddha!
please tell me—why do some
men take so long
to read a woman's mind?
how come he doesn't understand
I am ready to give him
everything!
why doesn't he just carry me home?
my primitive instincts have already
reached their peak
minutes ago
when he was smiling
at me!

I am listening to him
with all ears and eyes
doesn't matter, even if he
is saying 'bullshit'
he looks great
it feels great
he likes to talk

he keeps talking,
about his German Shepherd
I dream of
Shepherd, me, and him
by the beach
a beautiful selfie
on Instagram

he keeps talking
about a movie
I imagine
holding his right hand
in the theatre
wearing a long red gown
and he with a red bow tie
on the neck
of his shirt
holding my left waist

he keeps talking
about his dream home
I dream a queen size
blanket with flawless
floral embroidery, a bed
full of roses
the scent of strawberries
coming from
our bathroom
me and Tom Cruise!

he now brings up
the topic of family.
I keep dreaming
about our new family, too;
to hold them
'from this day forward
for better for worse,
for richer for poorer,
in sickness and in health'

he says, 'I escaped Italy last week
shooting is postponed
as my assistant is infected by the virus
and my dad, too'
and his words were
followed by a loud sneeze

as if a bomb had been dropped
by a drone, the heart of this queen was killed

now she is crawling to escape
the word 'quarantine'
is dictating her thoughts
hiding her fear, she asks,
'Have you been tested?'

he says, 'I will get tested tomorrow, but don't worry,
I have got a clearance certificate. Not a big deal!'

The Queen of Love is now smelling
hospitals, a single bed,
wrapped in a white bed sheet and

a saline drip hanging next to her
all the doctors and nurses around her
are wearing masks; her relatives, in tears,
saying their goodbyes
through a glass window

I move towards the exit
in a hurry

Tom Cruise comes closer and asks,
'when can we meet again?'
I fumble, 'no kiss, thank you'

Tom Cruise opens his arms
I scream, 'No hugging, thank you'

Tom cruise extends his hand,
I shake 'no handshakes, thank you'

The end of the story.

A Cow Date!

One

A cow dancing
on the grass
seemed to be in his ****king element.
As I was passing by
he moved his tail and groaned:
'Hamba'
If I was not mistaken, he even winked at me.

Two

He is sitting on the couch of a café,
as we were set up on a blind date. Oh!
I am now talking about a good-looking man.
He shows no interest yet
in the talk, or in the coffee.
I bet even Jesus doesn't know what he's got
in his head.

You know, as Einstein said,
'*whenever an awkward person*
enters the room,
every moment becomes an opportunity
for you to leave.'

Actually, I said this. I often express my very own desires
using big names
my mum buys Einstein and Bill Gates
very easily, but Karl Marx—no, a big no, never works.

Oops, I am on a date.
'Do you know how to wink? I learnt
from a cow the other day.
I can show you, if you would like!'

The man swings his legs,
which are wearing an expensive pair of shoes,
opens his uptight mouth and says:

'Umm, I am a bit shy, so I don't understand
your silly thing. I reckon we could discuss this
in my bedroom? My apartment is not far away.'

The reason that many women are single in this city
popped into my mind:
some men are too shy to talk,
but are very much ready to take their clothes off
before a stranger!

After the date ended, I received a photo of him naked.
What could I do but to send a photo
of that cow!
He was outraged, texting: *'You violated the privacy of a cow.*
Did you even get permission from the owner?
You can't trade in the body
of a naked cow. Jesus, this is so cruel.
A lawsuit is under consideration.'

Three

'Wake up. You talked too much in your sleep last night.
Get dressed, they are coming.'

I realised I had slept on top of many cows:
a printed bed sheet with a cow,
running naked—a white face, brown neck
and black back: three colours,
all together, side by side—
a multicultural cow
bedsheet
Mum received as a gift last week
from her Indian friend

'Hey get dressed, the potential groom's parents
are coming to see you'

'Mum, Bill Gates said "Cows are better than men.
A cow gives three litres of milk a day: some to drink,
some to make a living, whereas a man is a loss-making project:
they make you the bearer of their children,
and then they leave."'

'Sleep with the cow then, you don't deserve any man!!'

Loveshot

I am 18. With my two googly eyes,
I see my mother cooking lamb biriyani
for dinner

[*loveshot*]

aromas drift far and wide;

the news warns an evening of massive storms
are on the menu, too

[*moonshot*]

Mum heads to the shower
leaving the dishes for me

Miss-Gun
[*Some English speakers may find it difficult to understand, they often get
confused with Megan*]

I bring her pussycat *Miss-Gun*
from the couch to the kitchen
and let her spice it up,

Miss-Gun begins her mission
by knocking to the floor

a series of dinner plates, one by one,

not even sparing the baby pink one

the one I received
from my soon-to-be ex-boyfriend, 'Hurry'
*[Some English speakers may find it difficult to understand, they often get
confused with Harry]*

disaster! debris of the dearest ex
is on the floor
as if the moments of a collapsing Mayan civilization
were re-imagined by a cat

[moonshot]

my mother screams

from her bathroom
'*ki hoyeche ki hoyeche?*' [what's going on? what's going on?]

Mum, back in the kitchen,
cleans the mess

see, how casually a kitten
can make the world calmer

by breaking weather, breaking news,
breaking delicate things
in our home?

Miss-Gun and I are watching TV, relaxing

everyone seems tired now

tired of debating whether
an 18-year-old can have a boyfriend

[*moonshot*]

muted flavour, softened air
this teenager, oblivious

[*loveshot*]

Midnight Lover

You shouldn't set foot in my home
at midnight, Handsome Man!
My nightwear is dishevelled,
as are my bedclothes, and lust.
Everything is rumpled.

You want to know?

Come in the afternoon—if you must come.
We'll have coffee together and talk, and laugh;
I'll water the plants on the veranda, with your spoon
you'll touch
the heart of the mug;
the clinks will stir my soul.

My husband will appear
to ask "Do you need more sugar?"

Saying 'No thanks,' to him, you can tell
the coffee-mug
all your untold stories:
with every sip you take.

When you leave
there will be a hailstorm somewhere
in this town.
I will read the coffee grounds you've left behind
furtively
so that no one knows
We could spend all our coming afternoons

this way, couldn't we?
If you bang on my door at midnight
I swear by the Lord
we will become a story ourselves
of a room of lust!

Burn me,
But don't set my marriage
                    on fire, darling!

The Diary of a Clever Man

And I shield my wife from

Cold water
Cold weather
Cold war
Cold sore
Cold meal
Cold bed

And HOT men.

Underrated

Beauty is overrated
Career is overrated
Education is overrated
Family is overrated
Holiday is overrated

Only sex in 60s, underrated.

Love is overrated
Money is overrated
Netflix is overrated
Politics is overrated
Religion is overrated

Only sex in 60s, underrated.

Husbandlike

My next door neighbour
(who I can't figure out if I like or not)
is a successful entrepreneur

Who most people would find quite a character
Who one could write a book about
Who never invites me for a cuppa,
though my husband has received three invitations
(unless a few more were made in my absence)

As the rumours have it
this lady has four partners (husbandlike)
One for giving her children and
One to look after them
One to look after the house, doing chores, hosting parties
One to cook and look after the kitchen

Rumour has it that lately there are some troubles in the house over
the issue of which husband should join her in her late evening parties

Lately, she has been picking the relatively younger one
as he has energy and he doesn't fall asleep halfway through the party.
And he takes her home if she has fallen asleep or is drunk

She finds her youthful days reflected in the eyes of this man
She tells him to make her some love, and he makes love
and she gives him beautiful gifts every day!

What else can a man want? He gets brand new belts, shoes, undies,
and plenty of pocket money, and watches with diamond designs
What more could a young man ask for?

But the other three husbands are unhappy.

She loves her very first and oldest husband,
that's why he's been given the job
of reading bedtime stories to the children

She loves her second husband,
he likes to cook, that's why,
even on the weekend, he can be found in the kitchen

She loves her third husband, who is sick today:
going through some mid-life male menopausal crisis
He needs some rest,
so the very generous, kind, loving wife sent him for bed rest

She reassures all her husbands that she is not a carnivore,
but a loving woman who makes sure all of her men
are being treated equally

She is wise and she knows that mens' only ambition
is to bring children into this world and raise them
while women are kind enough to carry children in their uterus
At this age, she does not want any more children,
but she is not tired of loving; she gets excited by the art of lovemaking.
She desires to explore this space some more.

She doesn't think all men should be so desperate
to bring children into the world. Sometimes,

it's important that men put their career before their desire for children
The only reason she married her fourth husband
is because he seemed to be very focused on his career,
not on having children

She says, 'I don't treat men like goods;
men surprise me with their dignity and loyalty,
and they have great solidarity among them
All my partners (husbandlike) spend time together
On the weekend, they watch the Netflix series
'How to Please your Wife'
Third husband is a bit jealous of fourth husband sometimes
But I ignore it
You know, it's natural'

As if society should thank her for her generosity towards her men
and (wo)mankind!

She is not entirely sure about the motives of male activists
'Activism is good as long as it does not
put men under pressure to earn money,
when women can do it better than them.'
She told the interviewer boldy in a recent TV show—
as I watched.

Love-Lottery

Love is a lottery

You never win

Yet there is a hope that keeps us

ALIVE

You keep trying for years and looking for centuries and you never make it

Love is a lottery

Those who won it by chance

killed early

by heart or by bank

Let's not talk about it.

LOVER

Rules of Love

My eyes are hearing your footsteps
and my ears are glancing at you
My lips are walking on your body
and my nose is kissing your lips
in shock and in excitement
Everything turns opposite

as I try to visualize
him walking into this classroom,
and taking his seat
Through the window I see
an apple tree
where many apples fly towards the sky
and the sky drops down to the ground,
telling me again and again how stupid Newton was
How can my hands run towards your lap,
if you don't keep buttons on your shirt?
How can my legs tell you that they love you
if you don't spread your hands?

I don't want to go far
Just want to sit on your lap
Let me sit there after the lecture
if you are not stupid enough

Listen carefully, listen with your heart, listen to
my whispering
I have never been the subject of any rumours
Let me try today

so that an apple falls to the ground, the sky stays up above
and we float in the air

I will kiss your lips if your teeth are brushed well—no rush
We can go for a deeper one later when you are all prepared
It's not that we will kiss is the only deal
Another deal is that the door and the windows
must remain open so that
my friends and my enemies can watch this
So that no one ever dares to come between us

From today you will be known and pictured as mine

Period.

NB: I will get you mouth freshener on your birthday
which is next week, isn't it?
Even though you smell great, I have a particular brand
preference; I bought a full bucket of male mouth freshener
last year at the Christmas sale
for you. They must be used
because I love the smell
and because they will soon expire.

Haiku On My Engagement Day

You look so gorgeous honey
I don't care about money
How deep my love is you will see very soon

Love, where are you taking me
Paris, or Venice, for the fifth honeymoon?

If there is a WW3

If there is a WW3, I won't stop you from leaving me

I will get me a Rooster and a Hen
I will give them some space in my backyard for their play,
in the night, for them to make love

Then the hen will be pregnant
laying eggs
it will give me chickens

and plenty of
protein to survive

I will live without your love

You may have to live with regrets of leaving me,
free meals, free kisses won't be found anywhere
You may have to (please read 'must') live on stealing eggs
and chickens from my backyard

Your best bet will be to be the Cock on my couch
cuddled by a beautiful chicken

The chicken who dances on the couch wearing red lipstick
and gives a guard of honour
to her

True Lover.

Lover, Where Are Your Eyes?

Lover, where are you?

Lover, look at me, here I am

Lover, don't you have a toothbrush?

Lover, deodorants are on sale, can I get you one?

Lover, tell your mum not to call every single minute we are together

Lover, let's enjoy the night at the bar

Lover, where are your eyes?

Lover, leave me alone.

The Canola field

I am not your poem, honey
Don't wish to be read fully
I want you to read me only halfway
I wish to be your short story
Where they will never know the silly things
that made us
fall apart in the Canola field
beneath its yellow flavour

*If you ever write about us, the last line of the story must be left a
mystery that won't tell whether we grew old together or parted, never to
meet again, leaving behind the egos and partners with whom we wasted
our youth*

We danced under the moonlit night
fixed the tent before it got broken right
Haven't you heard of love at the first sight?
Half of me in the dark, and half in the light
I'll never let people know how our sweet kite
soared overnight.
Everything, everything, everything was so right
as the moon held us tight

*You can put me under your pillow like a story book and fall asleep
holding it, without raising any suspicion in the woman you are sleeping
next to. Every time you look at it, you see through me, every time you
read half of it, you can get lost in me, every page you touch relies upon
me, every word you write echoes me, even when I am not yours!*

Don't you come to me
Don't you finish reading me, my darling!
I am not your poem
A short story doesn't demand an ending;
let's dream only that we are having
the same drink for one more spring
to be sprung
for a while in the Canola field
beneath its yellow flavour

My next door neighbour's old harmonium keeps playing:
Sa re ga —Re ga ma— Ga Ma Pa—Ma pa dha—Pa dha ni—Dha ni sa
Sa ni dha—Ni dha pa—Dha pa ma—Pa ma ga—Ma ga re—Ga re sa.

Ass-tro-losers

I've been looking for a lawyer
to file a case

against a group of professionals

who have been telling me for the past five years
that I'd be in a relationship

Except for Netflix, no one has arrived
in my bedroom

I want to kill those fuckers
Liars
Losers

Officially, they are known as astrologers
I deleted all their contact details

before making a big decision today

I'm sitting in the reception area of my potential solicitor,
turning the pages of a magazine on their coffee table,
when my eyes get stuck on
today's horoscope:
'Stay away from legal issues, it may lead you to bankruptcy.
Romance inevitable.'

My solicitor—a young Hugh Grant—just arrived
and is smiling at me…

What shall I do now?

Let Them Go

Boyfriends do bring flowers
ice-creams, toilet rolls
rub your back with sunscreens
Then they kill your careers
FOREVER

Treat yourself tonight
If you
ARE
a single woman

Dance with every inch of your body
Pour yourself a glass of whiskey

Kill the cow before it gets you laid down

Or, let him run away naked.

Love 101: Self Help

Overwatering kills your lovely plant
Over-loving ruins your loves
And your living

Live and love with a measuring tape
on the table,
and next to your bed.

That's how those who died happy lived and loved.

HOME POLITICS

Some Mothers, When Not in a Movie

Mother is a mysterious darkness

who gets to write our history before we were born,
who picks the best man in town to be our dad, or doesn't get
to have a choice at all

As we are born, they fall apart
As our father goes to find and harvest a new spring,
she searches for him in us

As we grow, she keeps asking for her dues

All we can do is ignore her phone calls
Yet she will be the winner

One day, I will regret not taking her calls
if she passes away before me.

Mother is the biggest hijacker on earth

who we cannot put in a prison
as she emerges as a not-for-profit hijacking practitioner
who wants to snatch the happiness from one child—
the one who climbs the ladder of success,
or owns a fat bank account, or ranks high in society—
to give away some portions to her less happy
or needy child, siblings or relatives
(even if they are 50 years old!)

And she keeps returning like a beggar, as if nothing is enough,
never was, and the more you give her, the hungrier she gets

And she curses us in public
when we don't pay her a visit, but she doesn't forget
her prayers to God for our well-being in her solitude.

Mother is a wild rose

who wounds us with her thorns
as the flower of her youth has been stolen
by her marriage, children
after children
and making meals after
meals after meals;
meals after meals,
three times a day,
seven days a week,
fifty two weeks a year,
for all those mouths, for decades.

Mother is a lone democracy [demo-crazy],

elected and ruined by her unsuccessful child and a social system
that she will blame on others
We hate her political mind, divided heart, partial self
We hate her demands, not being herself.

Mother is a water lily

who carries us across an ocean, all alone, keeps us wrapped
in those stormy nights into her breast, dismisses our fear,
saves us from beasts, hidden and open, in and out
and in this long war, we eat her
sweet youthful flower.

A Letter to the Bin

I am not sorry that I told you all those lies:
missing school, missing exams, I spent day after day
in my dark room,
windows closed, door locked, crying and crying

I am not sorry that I forged your signature
many times
put it on the parents' approval letter
to the school. I am not sorry
as you never had the time or interest to approve
my excursions or school reports

I am not sorry that you tied my shoelaces
only once in my lifetime, and that was done incorrectly
and the whole school laughed at me. I am not sorry at all
as you were still with me, with us, under the same roof

I am not sorry that I can barely imagine your face
waiting at the school gate

You know what I remember? I reminiscence about the face
of the ice-cream seller with his little van just before the school gate,
as he was the only way to find a little comfort
But in those days, in grade five, I had given my pocket money
to the local mosque to pray
that you would come to pick me up on my sports day
At least once,
I wanted to show you all the prizes I received through the week,
but that wasn't your priority

I was desperate to show my friends that I had a dad
who cared a lot for me
And, you never showed up.
I told my friends, *'My Dad is abroad, that's why he can't come'*

By Grade 6 in a new school, I told friends that my dad died
in a car crash abroad
and he was buried there
My friends often asked me, *'What sort of car was it? Who was driving?'*

—Sigh! I don't know much, but I heard it was a lady driver

Burying your living dad is possibly harder than burying a dead one—
the hardest thing I have ever done

Here in London, it rains all the time in the winter
No one likes it
You know what I do? I float my tears on the rain
It helps to float those lonely tears and find them company

The funny thing is I met a boy today at the campus
who hates his dad
Listening to his stories, I said, 'Oh that's cool!'
He burst out in anger and left the table
I couldn't tell him,
it's easy if you know you hate your dad
because of his drinking habit
and you figure it out—no expectation
But it's sad when you love your dad
You were so close
and suddenly things changed
and you woke up into a new life

where you can't go near him,
can't talk to him, or you just
don't talk to him

I am sad, Dad. You are nowhere
to read my letters,
so this might go into the bin as well
But I feel like screaming—

'Could you please come back for just a glance? Can we count fireflies again together lying on those armchairs in our backyard on those blackout nights?'

I thread every night with weeping
Every night, I re-write my childhood

I am upset, Dad
Anger has destroyed our bond
We couldn't unlock even the simplest problem in the world
We couldn't solve it
Are you feeling that you were too rude to me?
Or are you still counting my mistakes?
I heard you were trying to reach me through my relatives. I will call your number to hear your voice, but before that you must answer one question:

'Why did you punish me for the things that didn't work out between you and Mum?'

If you can't answer, if you don't admit your mistakes,
you will never hear back from me
I don't know how to bring a dead man back to my life
I killed you in grade 6 to survive in school and to live my life

I am sorry that I can't be next to you when you are bedridden
and counting days

NB: I have a confession to make. The box full of mice you found
in the wardrobe and the jar of cockroaches in the kitchen of your
new luxurious flat was my work: a little revenge I took
But the thing you blamed me for, breaking your new wife's
make up box, that wasn't me
It was her maidservant,
She apologised to me secretly
I didn't want her
to lose her job, as I know the pain of LOSING

—Sincerely, Sonia, your lost (abandoned) daughter, 21 December,
2010, Lonsdale Avenue, London.

The Broken Bond

I haven't touched you
in the past six months;
you are no longer

needed

in my life, sorry, I didn't mean to be harsh
Trust me, I haven't replaced you
I haven't put my eyes on someone else
I might, though, if needed

No, no, it's not that you are old
You still glow like you used to
You still stand so high anytime, night and day

I remember

that summer evening
the very first time
I brought you home
I put you on my bed
starred at you

Your size was perfect

For a while, I couldn't resist,
you lifted my legs,
two straps on my two ankles
I looked in the mirror, remember?

Last night,
I went to the basement
That's where you're staying
since coronavirus hit our city
You are a fallen king
who lost glory overnight
What can I do, honey?
Working from home, meetings are online
nothing nothing nothing demands

you.

You're still so sexy, but you don't
serve any purposes,
oh! oh! oh! Dear corporate high heels!

Forgive me.

A Voluntary Statement About the Murder I Committed

I just killed an intruder in my house

It happened all of a sudden
I didn't know my hand was so strong
That it could take a life
with just a single hit
A single hit!

My hands are bloody
Believe me, it was not intended
It was self defence

This happened before lunch
I went to my garden to pick some fresh parsley
The intruder tailgated me
When I was chopping a cucumber in my kitchen, the intruder
kissed my neck,
close to my right ear
obviously without any consent,

I hit hard and he died
leaving my fingers full of blood
Believe me, I didn't use the knife at all

I wrapped the body in a kitchen towel and dragged it
to the big green rubbish bin

I washed my hands like an agent
I know there are some who might drag me to court
Do I really deserve to go to prison for this crime
when his gang is already punishing me further?

The intruder didn't leave me alone
as I sat on the chair before my lunch and found
two companions of the victim
singing and eating
my lunch

This time, before I moved my hand, they fled
and left two little eggs
of their heirs
on my plate

Never underestimate the power of flies.

Sex Party of Cockroaches

My kitchen is a Heaven for sex
Where overnight lovers make their best memories
on a soap-soaked scrubber
in my kitchen

And this great discovery diffused to the neighbourhood
when I am single!

A pair of cockroaches caught in my CCTV
over the weekend
in my kitchen

doing odd stuff on top of my dish scrubber
joined by some mates
Then others
Then others
in my kitchen

in different sizes and ages
throughout the night
those pairs kept going, a non-stop Sydney to Paris flight
in my kitchen

I have never watched any blue films
But, God has punished me this way
in my kitchen.

Song of a Fish

two little fish, eavesdropping,
one fine morning, they find it astonishing,

some artists singing love songs, and playing
at the lakefront of Tuggeranong, ping! ping!

enjoying the music, the female fish goes mad
she urges her lover to sing her a serenade

HE refuses and sermons, 'it's an an old problem, nothing new,
ah! honey! today they sing in public: "falling in love with you"

tomorrow they cry by the lake, all alone, see depression!
no wise fish sings such silly serenades but lives in elation!

stay away from these love debacles, just
dive slow but kiss me super super-fast!'

The Left-Handed

Being left-handed, they laughed at me
My classmates would ask, 'Which hand do you use
in the toilet
and which one to eat?'

My mum kept hiring private tutors
to train me to use my right hand
None of them were successful.

My Dad came home one day very excited
He called everyone as if he'd won a lottery
and announced what he had found
'An English daily has published a story
about left-handed people
that they are more brilliant than
right-handed people like us'

My uncle got furious and annoyed
He screamed,'Why do we have to believe these Westerners'
nonsense stories? Don't we know that the left hand belongs to the Devil?
Don't be fooled by believing an American conspiracy.
America and the Devil go hand in hand'

It's now 2008, I am no longer a child,
Many things changed but two remain unchanged
I am still a lefty, and am still getting humiliated for it
'Who will marry a devil-spirited girl? Any idea how odd this looks?
Why can't you just use your right hand?'

Barack Obama is waving his hand
on the TV screen as the 44th President of the USA
The news anchor keeps saying, '...the left-handed President
... the left-handed President'
I turn the volume high
I laugh at my uncle

My uncle is very upset these days because his DV lottery
application has been rejected by the USA
The last attempt he made failed as well,
It is so clear that he won't be able to pursue
his American dream

But I had to leave early to pack
for my flight to New York tomorrow.

SOLITARY SONG

The Best Dressed Woman

One

Scientists say 'brains respond to threats' and literary geniuses, for
centuries, have been selling us Cinderella stories:
the runaway girl who loses her sparkling glass slipper,
and the prince that finds her to give it back

Scientists say 'brains respond to threats' and psychologists have
been selling us evidence-based studies that we develop our
perception based on class and society [They forgot to include
Instagram and Kim Kardashian]

Has anyone come across studies about the pain of being
the best dressed woman in a room? [When they are not on the red
carpet of Cannes or the Oscars]

Or the pain of being the prettiest in a gathering? [When they are
not at the Met gala]

Or the pain of being the so-called privileged in a society? [When
they are not Royals]

She is alone, no Fairy Godmother exists these days.

Two

Strangers (men) randomly go the extra mile
to capture a moment with her
to make it look like
she slept with them last night
Her female friends often make sure
she is out of the group photos from last night
(unless an awkward moment
of her is being captured!)

Who likes a prettier woman smiling next to them?

Who wouldn't like to join in the gossip about how many men
she has slept with?

as if they were the witnesses,
as if they were underneath her bed when she was

fucking those men.

Three

Forget the dress and the attention of last night, today we will focus
on her achievements: how her beauty has grabbed everything she
is not supposed to have; discussion continues.

'*She has won a medal for brilliant academic performance. How come?*
Teachers must have favoured her,' one says.
'*Old professors like young girls. Who doesn't know that? Holy crap!*'
another says

'*Her professor was a woman,*' someone mumbles and no one hears

'*I wonder what she will do when she gets old and where her pride of
beauty will lay? No lover will get her that expensive dress!*'
Laughter burns the room; it echoes from the walls like deadly ghosts
As if they will never grow old, it's only she
who will outwear her beauty with age

Scientists say 'brains respond to the threats' and she doesn't know
what to do when
she is a threat, simply for a dress

that she bought for the bargain price of

$15

from a charity shop

No one knows, but she

dreams of losing
one shoe, at least for an evening.

Three Buds

A bud has bloomed tonight, and the other two
are yet to. They are excited to see
what their future will look like—
an exotic bloomed version

of them—their destiny—like clouds must give rain
one day—their dream—like a cascade must flow through the
mountain—their dream—to reach their peak—their dream—to bloom

The bloomed flower remains sad for a while
and utters 'I will be chopped off in an hour to be sold in a flower shop
Don't bloom sisters, take as long as you can—not to bloom.
Stay with mother.'

Dear Young Tree

Whisper me some truths
Who do you secretly fancy in the night: fireflies or bees?
Do you exhale when two rosy-faced lovebirds sit on your arms,
doing a poo-poo game and spreading it over your body?

At sunset, after the wind, your leaves float serenely on the lake
Do you mourn for your fallen leaves? Have you ever wished
to be a boat and follow their whereabouts? Do they go to
Adam and Eve?

Tell me your birthday and any wish you are longing for
Do you want a rain shower? In India, two frogs were married
to appease the rain God. I can arrange two frogs and set them
to marriage, and bring the Sky with its raining buckets down
for you. But, where do I get the Priest who will agree to this?
And who will be wedding guests?

Would it be alright if I am the only one?
A tree, two frogs, and me.

Grandpa-Grandma Drink

My grandpa would love to buy a bunch of sugarcane; under the setting sun in his back yard, he would peel and chop them off into little pieces and forward the bowl to me '*chew them, you will have nice teeth and a strong jaw*'. I would eat them like some medicine and would struggle the whole evening to empty the bowl. As night fell deeper, I would throw the uneaten pieces out through the window.

My grandma had a lemon tree next to her kitchen in the backyard. She would love fresh ginger and lemon tea and she would also make one for me. She would place the cup in front of me as if on one fine morning a grown-up guest had come to visit her after ages and was being treated in some special way. '*Ginger makes bones stronger and lemon gives you vitamin C. You need it every day*'. I would drink my cuppa like medicine. Can you imagine an ice-cream lover having ginger and lemon tea on a daily basis?

I still eat sugarcane 25 and a half years on. I still eat them as medicine. When I eat them, I dream of a long walk with grandpa, our shared giggles and laughter. I don't pay visits to psychologists, only to juice bars who sell sugarcane juice in the area. I still eat ginger and lemon tea and act like a gentle lady; I sit in the dining space, and sip without any noise as grandma would command. I get to see her, she is looking at me with wonder, as if I am the eighth wonder of the world. I feel calm and peace; heaven can't beat it.

I have discovered some fusions lately: lemon and ginger with sugarcane juice. It's marvellous. All in one. Sugar cane juice with lemon and ginger. Me, grandma and grandpa together— memories in one drink.

You Don't Know What You Are

It's a kind of affection, isn't it?

I, yes, I

Can not snack without you
Can not nap without you
Can not watch Netflix without you
Can not have family chat without you
Can not take my weekend cuppa without you
Can not watch rainfall without you
Can not see the sunset without you
Can not gossip without you

Do you even know what you are, my couch?

An Evening With a Celebrity

today I will share
with my lovely audience
the recipe
for drinking water

Step 1.
first, you need to wash the glass,
double check if there is any
smell of dish washing liquid
better to wash it off again
don't stress, you can make it

bear with me!

Step 2.
turn your tap on
hold the glass
right under it
not too close
not too far

prepare
yourself
to stop the tap

before the glass is spilled over
to avoid the waste of gold

Step 3.
now, place a small
round-size plate
under the glass

open your freezer
get some ice-cubes
drop them into your water

then hold the glass
casually
and sit properly
somewhere
drink softly, gently

without making any noise
you are not in
a refreshment area.
NO sound please!

ensure some etiquettes
with a slight break
take a deep breath
halfway

and finish it
(un)like you did on your first date.

Step 4.
the last but the most important
part is to take
a selfie

and let the W-O-R-L-D know
your unseen talent
of drinking water, don't be shy!

Step 5.
you can add some flowers,
napkins
for a romantic touch
in your recipe.

N.B., if you liked my recipe, don't forget
to subscribe to my channel! Next week,
I will be here with my award-winning recipe:
'how to drink milk'!

subscribe to my channel
subscribe to my channel
subscribe to my channel
subscribe to my channel
subscribe to my channel

Everything Ends

Only those who end it

Nicely
May call it a victory

Everything ends
Only those who don't end it

Forever

They begin

May it be the road of love or loneliness

See you there!

Notes

'Excerpts from Marilyn Monroe's Notebook, 1962': this poem was exhibited by the Tuggeranong Arts Centre (TAC) in 2020. It was written during a TAC Solastalgia poetry workshop with Melinda Smith.

'The Naked Eyes': first performed in 2016 at the Front Café & Gallery Lyneham invited by Ellie Malbon.

'A Caged Dentist': first performed in 2018. Thanks to Faye Brinsmead for her feedback on it.

'Love in the Time of Coronavirus': first performed on 9 March 2020 at Smith's Alternative, before Canberra entered lockdown.

'A Cow Date': first performed on 3 Feb 2020 at Smith's Alternative.

'Loveshot': first performed for *Poetry on the Move* 2020 online and on Valentine's Day at Smith's Alternative on 14 February 2022.

'Midnight Lover': was published on the *Australian Poetry Anthology* 2020, Vol 8, edited by Melinda Smith and Sarah Saleh. First performed in 2016 at a Multilingual Poetry event. Thanks to Imogen Brown, Arunava Sinha and Samantha Hartley for their feedback on the initial work.

'The Diary of a Clever Man' and 'Underrated': were first performed at Smith's Alternative, 14 February 2022. 'The Diary of a Clever Man' was also published on Facebook by That Poetry Thing.

'Rules of Love': first performed at Manning Clark House, 2019.

'The Broken Bond': an early version of this poem was first performed in 2020 at Australian National University (ANU) and published by an ANU literary magazine *Rabbit Hole* in 2021 as 'The Fallen King'.

'A Voluntary Statement About the Murder I Committed': first performed at Smith's Alternative, 2021.

'An Evening with a Celebrity' and 'Song of a Fish': commissioned by Tuggeranong Arts Centre, 2021, curated by Jacqui Malins and Aidan Delaney.

'Dear Young Tree': commissioned by the City Renewal Authority as part of the Haig Park Reactivation project in 2020, this poem is on display as a sign in Haig Park, Canberra.

'The Canola Field' and 'A Letter to the Bin': first performed at That Poetry Thing, Smith's Alternative, 2019.

'Three Buds': written in February 2024 during a Bankstown Poetry Slam workshop at the Sydney Opera House.

'The Left Handed': written during a poetry workshop in March 2019 with Joelle Taylor.

About the Author

One summer night in December 2011, Asha landed in Canberra airport from London. On her way from the airport to her accommodation, Asha felt unexcited and unhappy: the weather was too dry; the moon in the sky didn't look as big as it was promised to be in the Southern Hemisphere; people had gone on Christmas leave; the taxi driver played terrible music, and the city looked like a ghost town. She wished to return to London immediately thinking: 'This is a place where perhaps no poets could ever be born'. Little did she know that five years later she would be known as the 'Queen of Quirky' poetry. A small island's little girl someday would emerge as a big name in the literary scene of the capital of Australia.

Born and raised in Bangladesh, Asha wrote her first poem when she was an eighth grader (contrary to her loving Dad's memory that it was when she was a fourth grader). Despite publishing many poems in local newspapers and even receiving awards in literary competitions, she never published a poetry book in her native country. Australia, a multicultural nation, which prides itself on its diversity, now proudly presents to the world Asha's debut poetry book: *Lover, Where Are Your Eyes?*

Asha is a scientist and social scientist with two undergraduate degrees from the Australian National University: a Bachelor of International Security Studies and a Bachelor of Science. She also holds a MSc in Climate Change and Development from the Institute of Development Studies (IDS), University of Sussex, UK. She works in the cyber security industry. She also has experience working as an Advisory Board Member for the ACT government.

In her spare time, apart from poetry performances, Asha likes to pretend to be a fortune teller, a backyard singer and a relationship advisor. Rumour has it that her first piano teacher ran away due to her terrible sense of rhythm.

www.ingramcontent.com/pod-product-compliance
Ingram Content Group Australia Pty Ltd
76 Discovery Rd, Dandenong South VIC 3175, AU
AUHW020639050325
407891AU00002B/11